MAIDEN SPEECH

ELEANOR BROWN

Maiden speech

BLOODAXE BOOKS

ISBN: 1 85224 351 1

First published 1996 by
Bloodaxe Books Ltd,
P.O. Box 1SN,
Newcastle upon Tyne NE99 1SN.

Bloodaxe Books Ltd acknowledges
the financial assistance of Northern Arts.

Cover printing by J. Thomson Colour Printers Ltd, Glasgow.

Printed in Great Britain by
Cromwell Press Ltd, Broughton Gifford, Melksham, Wiltshire.

For SAB and Miss Jones

Acknowledgements

Some of these poems were included in a collection for which Eleanor Brown received an Eric Gregory Award from the Society of Authors in 1993, and some were first published in *The Gregory Anthology 1991-1993* (Sinclair-Stevenson, 1994).

Contents

Bitcherel

You ask what I think of your new acquisition;
and since we are now to be 'friends',
I'll strive to the full to cement my position
with honesty. Dear – it depends.

It depends upon taste, which must not be disputed;
for which of us *does* understand
why some like their furnishings pallid and muted,
their cookery wholesome, but bland?

There isn't a *law* that a face should have features,
it's just that they generally *do*;
God couldn't give colour to *all* of his creatures,
and only gave wit to a few;

I'm sure she has qualities, much underrated,
that compensate amply for this,
along with a charm that is so understated
it's easy for people to miss.

And if there are some who choose clothing to flatter
what beauties they think they possess,
when what's underneath has no shape, does it matter
if there is no shape to the dress?

It's not that I think she is *boring*, precisely,
that isn't the word I would choose;
I know there are men who like girls who talk nicely
and always wear sensible shoes.

It's not that I think she is vapid and silly;
it's not that her voice makes me wince;
but – chilli con carne without any chilli
is only a plateful of mince...

Tragic Hero

Self-styled reluctant womaniser; less
predator, he, than lost-boy-victim, yes?
Touchingly hesitant, he, to confess
that all his life he has been in a mess;

meanwhile, his gentle, adept eyes assess
the fastenings and workings of her dress.

And after her? Another her, to bless
his cotton socks, to soothe his loneliness,
to kiss his melancholy lips, to press
her undistinguished gift of a caress
upon him, whose high-seeming, strange distress

is permanent post-coital tristesse.

Gossip Mosquito

You may quite dislike the ingratiating whine,
but please, no sudden movements, no sharp slaps.
If you'll just let me settle close enough to touch,
we can be cosy; intimate, perhaps –
I've a little store of secrets to share (not mine).
Yours for the asking. I don't ask for much.

I can do it very delicately, you know.
A moment's quiet intercourse with you,
which will not hurt a bit, will make me so content.
Am I a louse, to stick to you like glue?
Before you feel the least swelling or itch, I'll go,
taking so little...what should you resent?

Don't brush me off, you sweet, shy thing. I only want
one tiny drop – oh, such a tiny drop –
one bead of confidence, one crimson confession,
to fill me up. I do know when to stop;
one needn't gorge oneself, in a good restaurant.
One learns self-restraint, in this profession.

Pity

It was fully an hour, I think, after you'd gone
when the image arrived at the front of my mind
that had lurked at the back as you talked on and on.

It was summer in Normandy (so far, it's kind)
– it was Wednesday – market day – one narrow street,
in a village like any not far from the sea,

where a lobster costs less than a sliver of meat
(and the oyster-man opened one up for me, free,
when I said I had never had oysters before,

and was friendly in French, so I had to pretend
it was lovely, but thank you, I wouldn't have more;
very English, this eagerness not to offend).

At the end of his stall, in their shallow white trays,
were the crabs. Still alive, of course – guaranteed fresh –
but, all brooding on fate, and the horrible ways

that we have of extracting their tender white flesh,
they were listless as warriors caught fully armed,
but unmanned by the prospect of death at the hands

of a captor so huge he can never be harmed;
and the claws that had terrorised Normandy's sands
were now feebly manoeuvred to sign 'I resign'.

Thus, dejected and helpless and lying in heaps,
they exuded a visual kind of a whine,
like the viscous emission that bubbles and seeps

from a bottle of something unpleasantly thick.
From a crevice – a mouth? – at the front of each shell
came a bubbling oozing. Not rabid. Not quick.

An occasional pop; a continual well.
Like the stuff we produce when we've cried all we can,
the catarrhal saliva that clings to our lips.

Like the trickling self-pity that renders a man
so repulsive our patience first frays and then rips
altogether – especially after a night

when we've sympathised, soothed and attempted a joke,
and been silent at last, when a silence seemed right.

Dying crabs, you reminded me of, as you spoke.

She should have been

She should have been a semi-precious stone;
a not entirely worthless stone, whose price
reflected its availability.
One capable of looking, oh, quite nice,
in any setting dull enough to throw
its limited appeal into relief.
But not of any beauty on its own.
Too little faceted, perhaps, to show
much brilliance or colour; not to be
the focal point in any ornament.
A rather dated silver brooch, perhaps,
might house a few like her around the chief
attraction. Or the kind of chain which snaps
like the thread of a worn-out argument.

Imitations of Immortality

Worms may come for her shining skin,
maggots for her blue eyes;
fungus may start where she is laid,
nudging between her thighs;
her golden hair may moulder away,
white teeth crumble to dust –
O, she may well disintegrate,
as human bodies must;
yet she will not surrender
to those voracious guests
(inviolable forever)
her perfect plastic breasts.

The Lads

The lads, the lads, away the lads;
we are the Boys, who make this Noise: hoo, ha; hoo-*ha*;
a-*way*, awayawayaway, a-way, away;
ere we go, ere we go, ere we go;
we are the Boys, who make this Noise:
hoo *ha*.

Away the lads. I love your poetry.
It strips the artform down to nakedness,
distilling it to spirituous drops
of utter purity.
I like the way you shout it all so loud,
revelling in the shamelessness
of its repetitiousness; the way it never stops
delighting
you. You've every right to be proud
of your few, brief, oral formulae –
any of which will do, for *Match of the Day*,
or Friday night, Lads' Night Out,
lagered up and fighting –
you are the lads. You've every right to shout.

Your poetry belligerently asserts
what nobody would trouble to deny:
that you are the lads; that there you go;
that yours will never be to reason why.
My unsingable songs cannot do more for me
than rid me of my epicene disgust,
after I've served you all ten pints and watched
you flushing up with random rage and lust.

You'll smack each other's heads tonight
and shag each other's birds;
you are the Boys, who make this Noise.
What need have you for words?

We will not argue, therefore, you and I.
Your poetry serves your purpose; mine serves mine.
You only tell me what I don't deny,
and I don't tell you anything. That's fine.

Away, the lads. Your deathless chants will be
heard in these bars and streets long after we
are dead (for lads are mortal too); your sons
will never feel the need for different ones.

The Oak Room

Three hogs, stuffed into three expensive suits;
of one dead branch, three bloated, stinking fruits;
three scabrous chunks of English Upper Crust,
one avarice, one gluttony, one lust;
slurred words brayed out between their flagging jowls,
drink-drowned lost consonants and ravaged vowels;
three hairlines, horror-stricken, flee away
from sweating brows and bloodshot eyes; pink-grey,
indulged and sagging excess flesh aquiver –
O grant them soon cirrhosis of the liver,
our English God! Whom, on our English knees,
we thank for public schools, and men like these.

Fifty Sonnets

I

First moments have a sweetness of their own,
by virtue just of being primary;
first glance, first conversation, first exchange
of wit, first careful, accidental touch
(and later on, of course, first time alone,
first access to your thoughts in privacy,
first tactics to familiarise the strange,
and so on). First, there doesn't seem so much
to warrant the initial fascination
(the reasons always come somewhat behind),
but some first things have power of a kind
to mock you out of easy expectation.
My measured utterance was ripped in half
the first time you threw back your head to laugh.

II

Six minutes' silence, as you first caressed
my hand, which was the tacitly received,
first, physical, deliberate, overt,
licensed acknowledgement of your desire.
Silent and still, apparently obsessed
by this, I watched six minutes (unrelieved
by commentary) slide past. Being alert,
more, I think, than you realised (a higher
self stands by, asking what we think of this;
observes each minute movement of your hand
at mine, is differentiating sense
from thought), in six long minutes' present tense,
there's little I can't come to understand.
Conflict. Decision. Provocation. Kiss.

III

When Dante first saw Beatrice, she wore
a red dress – probably not much like mine.
Allowing, though, for accident (design,
and taste, and length, and Lycra), what he saw
was more or less what you saw on the night
when I decided you were mine. My dress
was red in its intent and – more or less –
red in its consequence. And I was right
to wear it, and play "queen" with those poor boys
who didn't know quite what was going on,
and deferentially provided noise
of admiration and desire. These gone,
certain of these, and certain of your bed,
we left; and the rest is taken as read.

IV

As if you took a Virgin and a Christ
out of some gravely lovely Pietà,
had her deflowered, him unsacrificed,
and stripped them both – so, this is how we are,
when you lie sprawled across my sweat-soaked breast,
one arm outflung across the crumpled bed –
only a sated animal at rest;
only a boy whose mistress strokes his head –
in this most secular of states, your eyes
will scarcely see the odd profanity
(the tenderness you do not recognise
as mother-love for some dead deity):
      but I, with twice-corrupted innocence,
      fuck you, and fuck religious monuments.

V

I laugh in climax, and you ask me why
(jaws locked around my loosened consciousness,
as though at such a time I might be less
inclined to weigh my words, or tell a lie –
and I appreciate it's worth a try).
So, let me catch my breath, and somewhat after,
explain that climax, more or less, is laughter.
An answer not designed to satisfy:
darkly displeased, you'd like it more if I
called out, or gasped, invoked my banished God?
Which suppositions all receive a nod.
'I'd like to see you angry. Make you cry.'
A few cold words? Cheap tears? You should be much
more flattered that my laugh rewards your touch.

VI

You ask what brought me here – into your bed! –
Last-ditch attempt to find myself elsewhere
than in the narrow cloister of my head.
Apartheid victim – as you stroke my hair,
as you caress the curve from waist to hip,
and even as we kiss, some splintered part
of me is waiting for me with a whip...
Don't ask what brought me here. Where would I start,
to find the language for an honest answer?
Better you should assume my appetite
drew me to you, as music draws a dancer;
better you should assume there was no fight.
     Revolt against my segregating mind.
     Lust for oblivion. Which I do not find.

VII

Rigorous to prevent it; far too proud
to say I do it; not to say aghast
that it should come to this, this schoolgirl state
of idiot preoccupation, when
all day, all day it's trembling on my tongue
and only gritted teeth can keep it back,
and even then, at times, it's almost been
impossible – some rebel 'Have you seen...'
escapes in conversation – then, the crack
of the internal lash leaves that much hung
in the air – I name some absent friend – then
go, find an empty room, since it can't wait:
intolerable luxury – at last,
at last I can just say your name aloud!

VIII

Probably the most human thing I do,
apart from dancing; and the only time
I'm not engaged in finding words for you,
or for myself, or fishing for a rhyme.
'The perfect sexual experience'?
Perhaps you misinterpret my ideal;
ecstasy, angel choirs, no preference
of mine: the act, ridiculous and real.
      In retrospect, that first, unfortunate
and technically disastrous time, when we
were stripped of glamour, robbed of dignity –
my giggling fit, and the importunate
telephone, and your three-times-lost erection:
that time, perhaps, was closest to perfection.

IX

I don't know what you want from me. We talk
about a lot of things, but never that.
And if I asked, I'd break the tacit rules
of this as-modern-as-they-come affair –
this marvellous, no-strings, no-rules affair;
this minefield of exact, unwritten rules
surrounded by barbed wire of silence. That
is something of a pity, since we talk
about a lot of things, but I don't know –
and maybe never will, since if I asked
I'd break the tacit rules – quite what you want
from me – and minefields (modern ones) with no
strings (just barbed wire) we cross with care, unasked
questions buried, like so much else we want.

X

My caterpillar curiosity
that crept into your arms and took up there
a kind of temporary residence
wriggled this morning in its chrysalis
of unexpected warmth, and struggling free,
noted with brief alarm a feeling where
something had grown – an unfamiliar sense
about the torso (metamorphosis
must always shock these little crawling things);
and shaking out its damp, translucent wings,
what had been curiosity arose
to find a name – observing which, you gripped
both flimsy bits of coloured gauze and ripped
them off, with, 'Ah. You won't be needing those.'

XI

Tell me I'm beautiful, and bring me flowers.
Tell me I'm fascinating, and you've never
met anyone so witty or so clever.
Worship me; sit and think of me for hours;
speak me the language of idolatry.
Go off your food. Fall sick. Have sleepless nights.
Resign your freedom, and all other rights.
Be bored without me. Write me poetry.
Don't notice other women; or compare
them with me, in my favour, if you do.
Earnestly tell me I'm too good for you.
Tell me you love me. Love me. Tell me there
is nothing you would not do for my sake.
These, and other demands, I do not make.

XII

Conscious of some discomfort recently,
unable to identify the cause –
not headache, hunger, nothing I could see –
I put myself away behind closed doors,
and tested gingerly all areas
that might be harbouring the irritant.
On being satisfied that various
organs and limbs betrayed no element
of bruising or disease, I hawked and spat
to clear my throat: and, with a tinny sound,
the phrase 'I love him' clattered to the ground.
    Stuck in my throat and choking me. Just that
small, three-edged piece of shrapnel from the fight
between my reason and my appetite.

XIII

[handwritten: style, fashion]

Mode Biblical – as comes so readily,
in stressful moments, to a girl like me.
You cannot know (I doubt that you would care) *[handwritten: internal thought]*
how many roles you played as you sat there
while your friend did his best to crucify— *[handwritten: friend is Herod?]*
me. This was no surprise, from him – but I *[handwritten: enjambement?]*
did not expect the following, from you:
Herodian – 'Let's see what you can do';
mob instinct for the winning side, like 'Free
Barabbas!'; faux-naïf hypocrisy *[handwritten: artfully simple. childlike.]*
of Pharisees – your 'I don't understand's;
then the Pilatian washing of the hands;
indeed, I looked for more from you than this
Petrine denial, or that Judas kiss. *[handwritten: betrayal]*

[handwritten: relating to St. Peter's]

XIV *[handwritten: denial of Christ]*

Sudden. Not unexpected, but much too
soon; inevitable, but too complete.
And swift enough to take my breath away –
the sight of your free-fall in my esteem.
I made no fucking angel out of you.
If I thought hero-worship from a sweet
young thing were what you wanted, I should say
'Find one.' This was no silly sixth-form dream.
But, my contaminated darling, I
did think that all our (your word) tenderness
warranted more than one mute, spoiled caress.
What hopes I had in you were not set high;
but, watching them so utterly brought low –
I think they call this feeling vertigo.

XV

Articulated threat of an abuse –
your warning, 'It will end in cruelty' –
although 'it' was so nice – has been of use
less, I suspect, to you (dear) than to me.
Under the influence of your clever friend,
you tell me ('warm, receptive, tender' and
not so clever?) how this thing will end...
  Note (dear) this warm and tender little hand:
besides receiving, it can give, as well –
and gave your marching orders with the ease
of a caress, last night. Could you not tell
there are some limits to my aim to please?
  Invite your clever friend to tell you why
your warm young mistress said that cold 'Goodbye.'

XVI

One kiss to open; one to set the seal.
And in between, of course, kisses in their
Catullan thousands. One, first, to invite,
accept, affirm, and breed desire for more;
one a full-stop, in showing you the door.
One eloquent, establishing the right
to trace your jawline, stray into your hair;
one taciturn – no rights, no tongues, no deal.
One trembling and expectant, through a smile;
one firmer and unyielding, through a wall
made of decisions made beyond recall.
One to say, 'I am yours now, for a while';
one, 'I am *not* yours now. But I have been.'
And in between? Oh, God – and in between.

XVII

That was, indubitably, not my voice.
Certainly that was not my voice I heard;
I don't care whose it was. It wasn't mine,
that quiet, rather frigid voice that said,
'What we will, for convenience's sake,
call *our affair*, is over. Nonetheless,
thank you for everything.' What voice was that,
that chilled the air around me as I sat
on the edge of the bed? What voice said 'Yes'
when you said, 'Then I'd better go'? I'll stake
my life it wasn't mine. Because my head
was filled with my own voice – a rising whine
of 'Stay, and let me love you' – not one word
of independence, finishing, or choice.

XVIII

It makes me wonder what you had in mind;
what personal, exclusive cruelty
you were devising, sweetheart, just for me.
Would it have been exquisite and refined?
Or wholesale and obliterating? An
ecstasy of humiliation, or
basic brutality? Me, on the floor,
begging as only broken women can?
    I'm not entirely ignorant of violence.
I never learned to like it – but I know
what happens when the vitriolic flow
of insults chokes itself into a silence.
    My last love taught me how to dodge a fist.
You could have tried to hurt me. You'd have missed.

XIX

My silence was, you said, 'not humanist'.
My absolute refusal to discuss
this was 'not humanist'. Perhaps I missed
something, somewhere, between the two of us?
    Perhaps you did. Before my inner eye,
two thousand years process – of bloody wars,
atrocities, the Inquisition, laws
most viciously enforced, Crusades and high-
rank nepotism, corrupt priests and Popes...
I, humanist? One of your fonder hopes.
    I might have been, some centuries ago,
branded a whore, burned as a heretic,
drowned as a witch – but I was, even so,
from soul to crown a Roman Catholic.

XX

Another night of sitting here like some
caricature of an old miser who
huddles hunchbacked counting the little store
of coins he'll neither gamble to engender
others, nor spend in the pursuit of pleasure.
Not even legal tender any more,
most of those coins; their status as a treasure
wholly dependent upon his obsession.
    Those phrases of no longer legal tender-
ness you carelessly left in my possession:
odd how significant they have become.
Night after night I sit and think of you,
weighing those phrases time and time again;
prodding my worthless savings with my pen.

XXI

Stillborn; aborted; cot-dead; premature;
dead on delivery; 'untimely ripped'
(not from the womb, perhaps, because I'm not
yet sure I've got so generous a thing)
or springing fully-formed out of my head,
in technical perfection – but quite dead.
Frost-bitten fruit; small victims of freak spring
snow; bud-nipped blossoms. All because of what?
Because I was not loved. Neglected; tipped
out with the bathwater; refused a cure;
exposed, as infants were who were the wrong
sex; drowned like litter-runts. You too, poor song:
like all these bastard progeny of mine,
you'll be garrotted at the fourteenth line.

XXII

Tonight ingenuous and generous
oblivious desirable forgiving
also imperative and dangerous
and burning steadily in love with living
sweet-limbed bright-eyed smooth-skinned and crimson-lipped
heady as conversation over drink
also inconsequential having slipped
out of the reach of conscience and I think
perhaps remorseless certainly no more
than ever willing to forego the right
to laugh looking for somebody to pour
this brilliance over O I am tonight
young lovely insolent and flown with wine
and this might all be yours. If you were mine.

XXIII

What do I have, when I contemplate this,
more than the knowledge that something has passed?
Something untruthful and warm as your kiss;
brilliant, brief, and too lawless to last;
free as gratuitous violence, and
serious, laughing and dark as your eyes;
rare as your compliments, deft as your hand;
highly desirable, highly unwise;
something that summoned me out of my state
(where I was happy) of being alone;
something that happened too soon or too late,
yes – but it happened. And it is my own.
What do I have? This intangible stuff.
Little enough – but though little, enough.

XXIV

Italians say it satisfies a man
to see his enemy before his feet
upon the ground – but that a woman can
never consider her revenge complete
until she has approached the supine form
and given it at least one damned good kick.
And Nietzsche says that after every storm
of bitter words, when conscience starts to prick,
a man is always troubled by remorse
to think, 'I may have hurt her; been too rough',
whereas a woman's torment is, of course,
suspecting that he was not hurt enough.
These sayings may not merit close attention –
but possibly, my love, they're worth a mention.

XXV

And yet I would have loved you. (If I don't
put that at the beginning, it may not
find its way in at all, which really would
be something of a pity; it's as true
as any of the other things that won't
be said now, and far nicer than a lot
of them.) And having put it down, I should
do what I actually set out to do:
say all the things that were to have come first,
like how I wanted you to prove me wrong
and win me back; and how, instead, each day
you disappointingly confirm the worst
of all suspicions. But the foolish song
comes out, I would have loved you, anyway.

XXVI

Not how or when, but where did I love you,
with that odd, shadowed love that never came
to anything? Somewhere without a name,
that isn't charted, and is not to do
with streets or buildings, cafés where one sits
and smokes and talks, nor rooms with doors that close
and beds one lies in; all of these one goes
to, sure of words, results or benefits.
    But where insistent waves of fantasy
fall in and foam upon the blameless shores
of more prosaic memory, and where,
blurring the sharp edge of reality,
possible things well softly up, and pause:
improbably, I loved (and love) you there.

XXVII

And what about the ones I didn't write?
And what about the ones I wrote, and then
made a fist round, and crumpled to a tight
ball, dropped on the floor, never wrote again?
The lines I tentatively wrote, and crossed
through with more certain, tight-lipped, swifter lines?
Ones that came on the edge of sleep, and lost
themselves by morning, leaving only signs
of their past presence in a half-formed phrase?
Ones that began so fresh, and were so staled
by the exhausted end of the same day's
drudgery? Ones I tried to write, and failed?
The ones that spoke with urgent honesty
(and were destroyed) of what you were to me?

XXVIII

Throw enough dirt on top, and it will pass
for something dead and buried in the end.
That's the approach. The reproach, I ignore;
it's feeble to begin with, anyway,
and all it takes to choke it is one day
of spadework. And the more I do, the more
adept I get at it – until I bend
double to call the sweetest moments crass,
to see the selfishness in all the most
innocent words, and call myself a fool,
and you a liar and a fool. That said,
I can survey my handiwork, and boast
how I, pragmatic, premature, and cruel,
buried a love that wasn't even dead.

XXIX

Just the touch of your fingers upon mine
(lighting a cigarette) and I have been,
just for a moment – anyway – a queen;
only a moment – just the space a line
might do for the expression of – and yet,
recalling how your hand was cupped around
my own – and then the slight, but noted, sound
of my breath changing – and my cigarette
not being very steady – I must be
conscious of this: that lecture as I may
'This thing is *over*', there will come a day
when you – perhaps in boredom – reach for me,
and I, though full of frigid wisdom now,
will know I should refuse, but not know how.

XXX

Having encountered you again today,
the selves are at their war again. I thought,
after a month or so's uneasy truce,
I might at last have seen them reconciled.
Poor ostrich hope. A month of quiet may
be time for sullen anger to be brought
to such a recklessness as to produce
threats of its own, break curfew and run wild.
      Thus, one insists on loving you, and cries,
'I shall betray myself, and you!'   'Absurd;'
replies the one who sang the Requiescats
over that love: 'forget him. Dry your eyes.'
'I *can't* forget!'   – But this is not a word,
this 'can't', to use in front of autocrats.

XXXI

he has accused her of fantasising of their rel.

1. Well, then – if it was only fantasy, a
2. it's been unusually durable. b — *contradicting here.*
3. Also far less easily curable b
4. than many of these things turn out to be. a
5. But now it's over, and I've lost you. And, a
6. now you sleep in somebody else's arms, b
7. I've nothing but my fantasy, which harms b
8. no one, and comforts me, you understand. a

VOLTA 9. — The facts? They only reach me by report. c
10. It's <u>circumstantial</u> <u>evidence</u>. They saw d
11. her hands slide up inside your shirt – no more.. e   *can't bear to hear the gritty truth.*
12. that's circumstance enough, I would have thought. e
13. So now I lie alone, and fantasise – d
14. dark, wordless dreams, in which she slowly dies. e

Signifies he tried to deny it

XXXII

Imperial, funereal, or both:
I wanted it to wrap around me then
(which you would not permit) and want it now
(which you cannot prevent) to keep me warm.
Deep, rich and sombre; solemn as an oath
must once have been, when oaths were used by men;
I understand why you could not allow
the studied monochrome and clean-edged form
of any of our conversations to
be swathed in this appalling colour, splashed
with these old, lurid shades. In some ways, you
were always careful. I am unabashed
without you – vulgar now, beyond restraint,
I'm running wild with purple, purple paint.

34

XXXIII

Wings, flames and arrows? Storms, and crowns, and chains?
Sighs, tears and throbbings? Death? One perfect rose?
All the fantastic trappings; all the old
tried trusted true trivial trite but true
accepted, true, rejected, true, much-sworn,
forsworn, outworn, ill-fated, dated things,
that *must* some time have sounded real and fine –
maybe it is a foolishness of mine
not to say simply that my heart took wings;
burned with desire; shattered before your scorn;
would willingly have made a king of you,
if not a god; saw life in red and gold...
a foolishness to say that I suppose
I underwent the normal aches and pains.

XXXIV

Two hearts cannot conjoin, when one of them
is artificially constructed out
of torn-up books, and stitched from neck to hem
with other people's words, and edged about
with tired, old-fashioned lace of borrowed sighs,
and when the other's purely functional,
does what it ought, and sends the right supplies
of blood through every vein with punctual
efficiency, and either ignorance
of, or indifference to, metaphor.
    Two such organs, even in innocence,
could never beat or break together; nor,
indeed, just meet – unless to stand apart,
and stare, and say, '*That* calls itself a heart?'

XXXV

I'm an old woman now, my dear; you've long
since been forgiven for the little pain
I suffered at your careless hands. You see
my own: they're peaceful, folded in my lap
or busy at my knitting; the wild song
my body sang with yours is a weak strain
distantly pulling at my memory.
That's going, too: I sometimes think, 'That chap –
bless me, what *was* his name? The handsome lad,
a bit like Linda's eldest – nice dark eyes –
I wonder what became of him? We had
some times, though, didn't we!'
                             But these are lies.
I'm no old woman yet. And if I were,
face, name, pain – none of it would be a blur.

XXXVI

How many miles are you away from me?
I haven't counted yet – but anyway,
it doesn't matter. Distance in mere miles?
It hardly counts for anything, these days;
not with the telephone and fax machine,
cheap travel, discount airfares, thin blue sheets
you have to cramp your writing on, to get
your longing sent by airmail – you can see
mere miles are quite discountable today.
      Strung up on silent wires, among the piles
of unused sheets, and fifty other ways
to count this distance nothing, I have seen
a quarter-year of days sail past like fleets
of empty ships. One can't discount that yet.

XXXVII

'In memory, we usually improve',
you wrote – 'It's better for our images'
to be apart, while kindly hours remove
the irritations, and the damages
that daily contact caused to the light bloom
of our first pleasure in each other! Sure.
You take my 'image' into the dark room
of six months' separation – and, secure
in your false science, touch it up to make
it look a little less like me, and more
like what you'd like. And mount your lovely fake,
when you've eradicated every flaw:
what better way to spend a half a year?
I want you as you are. I want you here.

XXXVIII

Come back to me, before some other voice
can come and drown your memory of mine
far off; come here, before some fresher tone
can overcome whatever tones mine had
that pleased you once; come soon, before a choice
is put to you, for come what may, the line
I hold you by will become frayed; my own
voice, distant now, can only come in sad,
small doses – always similar – 'Come back
to me, before I cease to matter – come,
come now, before you cease to feel the lack,
or come to find it bearable – or some
day soon, come, anyway – and when you do,
maybe I'll come some way to welcome you.'

XXXIX

I'm not cut out for tragedy, I find.
Speeches I learned by heart at seventeen,
and practised in my bedroom till I cried
real tears of spiritual sympathy,
now leave me cold. Perhaps my coarsened mind
cannot now scale those heights, or take the clean,
thin air, so dizzyingly rarefied.
Perhaps those scenes were never meant for me.
      Rewrite yourself, I tell myself. It's clear
that script is not for you; pick up the one
(in prose) which has him simply disappear.
The only speech you get is this: 'He's gone.'
      It isn't much. Word perfect now, I say
it rather well, and several times a day.

XL

When I recall you – as I often do –
between two paragraphs, against my will
(I try to keep you in parentheses,
but you will interrupt my reading as
you did my careful life, appearing through
the ruptured print to laugh at it), I still
hold the book open; part of me still sees
the page; but all my concentration has
swarmed to the memory of moments when
we sat and talked in other company;
and through a comment, every now and then,
the sudden, private glance you cut to me,
the flicker of amusement in your brow,
shredded my gravity, and shreds me now.

XLI

This is the letter that didn't get sent;
this is the tone that I couldn't convey;
these are the words that the other words meant;
these are the ones I was trying to say;
trying and failing and starting again,
matting the floor with rejected attempts,
writing, diluting, disguising, and then
losing in lying conditional tense:
save me from solitude. Come to me now.
Give me yourself. You should only be mine.
Teach me to hold you by showing me how.
Give me no words; I need only a sign.
Make me no promises. Ask me for none.
This is the letter, when all's said and done.

XLII

Not if you crawled from there to here, you hear?
Not if you *begged* me, on your bleeding knees.
Not if you lay exhausted at my door,
and *pleaded* with me for a second chance.
Not if you *wept* (am I making this clear?)
or found a thousand different words for 'Please',
ten thousand for 'I'm sorry'; I'd ignore
you so sublimely; every new advance
would meet with such complete indifference.
Not if you promised me fidelity.
Not if you *meant* it. What impertinence,
then, is this voice that murmurs, 'What if he
didn't? That isn't *his* line of attack.
What if he simply grinned, and said, I'm back?'

XLIII

He is a very inoffensive man;
a man without grave faults or dreadful tastes,
who need not be embarrassing; who can
tell an amusing anecdote; who wastes
less time than most on foolish flattery,
without descending into boorishness;
can pay a compliment quite prettily,
avoiding many kinds of clumsiness;
a very inoffensive man indeed;
an interesting man, and sensitive;
the sort that would be pleased to soothe a need,
if it were anything that he could give;
and I have sat with him this whole day through,
and hated him, because he is not you.

XLIV

The reason why the rich are idiots
is obvious enough to me by now:
riches are not considered, but enjoyed.
Enjoyment hasn't much, if anything,
to do with thought, or the insidious
examination that corrupts the brow
with anxious lines; the rich are not annoyed
by reason. Only poverty can bring
us wisdom to desire a better state,
and cause us (sensibly) to see our lot
as insufficient, whereupon we hate
(cleverly) those who have what we have not.
    Cold months of beggary taught me this rule.
    When I was rich in you, I was a fool.

XLV

Some day, when I have time and energy,
I'll go through all of this with a red pen,
eradicating everything I see
that separates you out from other men.
Some day I'll make this utterly detached
from circumstance, destroying any clue
or trace that might be recognised and matched
to one man in particular; to you.
Then I will claim I never loved at all;
I never suffered; I imagined it;
I'll say it was invention; I shall call
it freak production of an idle wit.
And I shall be believed. But I will know,
unfortunately, that it was not so.

XLVI

When you return, I'll tell you everything:
the anecdotes that I've been putting by
against the day I see you next; the small,
amusing things that happened all the time
you were away. Assuming you will bring
your old appreciation back, and I
will not have lost my wits by then, or all
my power to amuse. And whether I'm
girlishly glad to see you, or reserved,
expansive or contained, you will receive
all of those stories which are laughable –
except the best ones, which are unpreserved:
of nights I lay unable to believe
that so much misery was possible.

XLVII

What little of your heart I once possessed,
I joined with mine; which only made it more
painful to have the whole torn from my breast,
since it was slightly bigger than before.
Well, never mind, I told myself: put in
plenty of platitudes and you will see
it heal (not knowing how I should begin
to treat this space where both our hearts should be).
And so I tried – and in good faith – to fill
it up with common sense; and only found
this burned away the edges, so it still
gaped at me, only wider. It may sound
contrived, but it is there – and how it smarts –
a hole, greater than the sum of the hearts.

XLVIII

It was a custom with the sonneteers
to offer certain immortality
in payment for uncertain carnal bliss.
There may be nicer ways of saying this:
if so, you do it. Claiming poetry
insured against the damages of years,
they whined, 'Be mine – and when the wrinkles come,
the neater lines on this enduring page
will fix you permanently in your prime.'
And possibly the promise held, for some.
We know, who live in this enlightened age,
poetry makes nothing happen. But time
makes the same things happen as it did then.
'Be mine,' I say, and start to count to ten.

XLIX

Born in a time when you were fed the lie
that only irony was humour, you
may find this short on laughs. It doesn't do,
to double up and laugh until you cry
at something which is just ridiculous –
a merely funny joke. Nor to appear
shocked by the merely shocking things you hear,
astonished by the merely fabulous,
or touched by the merely moving. These last –
sentiments which you'd say really belong
to the lyrics of a popular song –
should, in fact, leave you just a bit aghast.
    And when I find these songs are popular,
I'll laugh with you, and say how right you were.

L

No fellow-mourners in this loss – since how
is such a loss to be explained? No call
for coffins, no last rites, no pyre, no grave,
no one who wouldn't giggle if I said,
'Help me to grieve for the death of my dream;
or at least send a tactful little card.'
    But do believe that such a loss is hard
to live with; and that constantly to seem
unmoved by it is hard; that what is dead
is dead because of you, so to be brave
and still generous is hardest of all;
you – caused the dream, were it, killed it, are now
murderer suicide and still my dear
and still, I say you were a good idea.

Out

Strip her first of home and family;
erase surname and address.
Second, dismantle national identity;
take away passport, language and race memory,
if any.
Leave her the clothes she stands
up in, and a little black dress –
indispensable, haw haw. No, no – not a penny.
Take off the blindfold; untie her hands.

Your name is no name.
You are no one's daughter, sister or wife.
No friend wonders where you are;
no lover dreams of you at night.
No, we can't help you. This is not a game;
it's a serious business, all right?
Never heard of it. No idea how far.
Really? What a shame.
Still, that's life.

One moment, miss.
Before we leave you, a quick check
to make sure the job's been done
thoroughly. Do you recognise this?
Or this? Do you rec-
ognise any of the following names: Christ,
Shakespeare, Beethoven, Rembrandt? None?
Excellent. Do you know what 'Zeitgeist'
means? The sun:

does it orbit the earth, or vice versa?
What is the penalty
for breaking the law of gravity?
What is the difference between Asia and Ursa
Minor?
Who wrote Montaigne's Essays? Where
is Mother Nature's vagina?
Can you name one famous fashion designer?
All right, gentlemen, I think we can leave it there.

Essex Girls

The jokes were many and short-lived.
No one remembers them now.
Mainly to do with your sexual ease –
sour with envy or fear,
under the sneers.

And these unlovely Romford streets
I see you stalking, undeterred,
high-breasted, from thirteen to twenty,
terrible in certainty,

thoughtless of the sturdy fruits
you'll bear to undeserving mates
too soon.
East Saxon maidens, make the most
of it, who flower early,
and gloriously, and briefly.

Prelude

& rising from your bed, & since, I keep
thinking of other kinds of rising: song
in the throat, welling up & spilling out;
dazed creatures waking from hibernal sleep;
aspiring flames; tense coils, depressed too long,
that suddenly spring up; the swelling shout
of crowd anticipation or applause;
    these, rising from your bed, & ever since,
still other kinds of uprising: the surge
of peasant fists against an unjust prince;
the wordlessly incessant upward urge
of insurrection at outmoded laws.

Mazurka

caught in the act last night a sudden wish
to be, for once, not inarticulate
in it; caught – unable to act, or fish
for subtle phrases; only, accurate,
clumsy, between taut breaths & quite unthought-
out, 'I love it!' comes hurtling down at you
from above – a wild throw, but neatly caught.
    & the delight, of saying something true.

Étude

Warmer than death, stiller than life,
sleep has you, if I have not.
& what if you are not mine?
Not mother, sister, daughter will ever see you so.
　　Let me a moment before you wake
study you; fix in my mind
before we make love, talk, rise
& put on names, clothes, manners, that this
is mine.

Waltz

Final embraces that taste even ultimate;
fierce as the night was seized, urgent & intricate;
shot with the consciousness 'we have been intimate' –
skirting the issue, how nonchalant, delicate,
laughingly, reelingly, visit me, *do* visit,
thinking it haltingly, slowly in triplicate,
this is goodbye is it, this is goodbye is it,
this is goodbye, is it?

Terrible Sonnet

—speaking to herself.

Tonight, again? Please, not again tonight.
Please close your eyes, for once, when I close mine,
soul; do not look for things to talk about.
Please do not argue, scold, discuss, suggest,
present the cases, represent the best;
particularly, soul, please do not shout.
And you, my foolish heart, please do not whine.
Just regulate your beating to the right,   *— engeurbeaur.*
and proper level for an eight-hour sleep:
believe me, it will comfort you far more
than anything from my exhausted store
of platitudes. If nothing else, just keep   *— memory.*
it for another night, and let me see
what it is like to sleep. And dreamlessly.

dull, insipid, banal remark.

50

Why him and not you

Because he never claimed to know me,
or my tastes, or how to gratify
them. Because he only said that if I
allowed him, perhaps he could show me
how happiness was.
Then, because
he exercises his imagination
on imaginary things, and not on me,
whom he likes to touch, and smell, and see.
Because he dislikes complication
(the sillier sorts)
and his thoughts
are usually set in the here and now.
Because his hands are dexterous and warm,
appreciative of texture and form.
Because I am neither his Sacred Cow
nor his Destiny.
Because he
is as happy with quiet as with
talk, and can be silent in a way
that leaves room for anything I want to say.
Because for him, a myth is a myth.
Because for him, a star
is a star.

Your Cake

Mother is drunk on tradition, her competent hand
sunk to the wrist in the rich mix
of your wedding cake.
I have gone mad for the words that go into your cake.

Latin butyrum; Old English butere;
thick primrose-yellow fat.
And (Arabic) sukkar: sweet and crystalline.
White, when pure.
Side by side on the kitchen counter,
the garnets, rubies, diamonds and gold
of our discarded engagement rings,
not to be made sticky; suddenly no more precious
than the words that go into your cake.

Fold in the beaten pale gold liquid
released from the hard membrane of the oval body
laid by the female bird,
containing the germ of the new individual.
Old Norse egg, superseding Old English ei.
Fold in the sifted, fine, soft powder,
flour of huete: the flower of the wheat.
Mother is feeling 'very Medieval'...
not as old as the words that go into your cake.

This is a giggle. In goes the treacle
(originally, a salve, alexipharmic or antidote;
hence, a name for a sovereign remedy),
shiny, thick syrup, black-brown as a beetlecase.
And the yellow rind of an ovate fruit with acid juice;
Middle English lymon, medieval Latin limo.
Crushed kernels of a sort of drupe,
(in Latin, amandula); sweet grit of ground almonds.
I am in love with the words that go into your cake.

Had you married a thousand years ago,
Mother and sister must have laughed similarly,
mixing with grease-glistening fingers

substances very like these,
an old, old notion of a celebratory sweet;
too rich for everyday, too heavy to turn with a spoon.

Vanilla! The 'little vagina'. Latin, for sheath.
The aromatic essence obtained from the slender pod.
If the silk of your wedding dress had a scent itself,
it would smell like this.
The folds of its waiting skirts
are vanilla-coloured.

Fold in the spices, tastes of the tropical isles,
wicked foreign aromas, worth themselves in gold-dust:
cassia, cinnamon, coriander, ginger, caraway, nutmeg, cloves.
Hebrew kesiah and kinnamon, Latin coriandrum;
ginger, after an etymological odyssey longer
and stranger than any mere physical journey
to root it out: from Sanskrit çrngavēram,
the antler-bodied foot.
Ancient, far-fetched, the words that go into your cake.

Old Spanish alcarahueya, from Arabic al-karwiya,
seeds of the umbelliferous Carum Carui:
caraway, yields a spice and a volatile oil.
Nutmeg, the musk-nut (Roman, nuce muscata),
got from the heart of the fruit of the evergreen
Myristica Fragrans.
Clow of gilofer, nail of the clove-tree;
the pungent, small, hard things were flower-buds.
Mystical, fragrant, the words that go into your cake.

Now it is time to subject it to heat.
Mother is nervous, confronted with alchemy:
'This is the bit that I can't control',
and murmurs a prayer as she pushes it into the oven.
So many beautiful words to be baked.
A wonder a tin could hold so many.

I am glad you are marrying.
Forgive me: I wanted to write you a sacred song,
such as maidens sang for their sisters' weddings
– io hymen, hymen io –
but I made a cake of it.

Beauty and the Prince Formerly Known as Beast

He likes to do the kind of thing that shows
his fine hands to advantage, when he knows

he's being watched. He paints on silk; he plays
the harpsichord or lute, although his gaze

is always on his polished fingernails;
when meals are ended, now, he never fails

to glance around the dining-table, shoot
his cuffs, select and peel a piece of fruit

with elegant dexterity...discards
it, after, and suggests a game of cards.

The fashion is for shaving very close,
and unplucked eyebrows are considered gross.

Men wear their hair tied neatly back, or short.
Hunting is rather frowned upon, at court,

though there has been a certain renaissance
in verse, theatricals and formal dance.

He dances consummately well. We make
a lovely-looking couple, when we take

the polished floor together. Later on,
the thousand candles snuffed, the guests all gone,

he'll take my hand in his, apply a slight
pressure with his cool lips, and say goodnight.

Then I remember how he looked at me
under that curse, when I would go to bed,
deep-set eyes burning in his shaggy head –
he used to look at me quite hungrily.

With this most gentle of all gentlemen,
it would be wrong to ask for that again;

I don't. But on my own, some nights at least,
I lie and wish, a little, for my Beast.

Mantis

Let me store some of the cells
from the skin of your shoulder
under my digging nails: sweet,
you will slough them off
(we are told) soon enough.

And, as it wells
up in your mouth, some saliva.
That I take neat,
though Medicine affirms
it's full of germs.

Seven years from this moment in time,
they say,
not an atom of you will be mine
that's mine today.

Then shed yourself if you must.
But I would not have it turn
into common dust,
as we lately learn.

All that I can feel here, and taste,
I oppose its disappearance.
If you'll give up old cells for new
in a natural system of clearance,
give them to me to keep, for I cannot bear
an iota, a drop, a hair
of what is you
to go to waste.

Leda, no Swan

Where I'm not given a complaisant smirk,
my mouth might be a slightly startled 'O' –
a half a 'no', that needn't count as No.
You will deduce he didn't have to work
so very hard, to part my pretty legs.
His curving neck, my curving arm, his beak
in almost a caress against my cheek –
no, this is not a scene, you'll say, that begs
use of the hard word Rape. Where is the rape?
Look how the gentle victim's dreamy eyes
register nothing more than 'vague' surprise;
those limbs suggest no effort at escape.

Ever been frightened by an animal?
Ever get knocked sprawling flat on your back
in the senseless impact of brute attack?
Ever been winded, *and* hysterical?

Wings that could break your arm thrashing your chest,
a black bill hissing in your eyes, obscene,
inhuman, spitting noises that can mean
nothing but let-me-get-it-in; you, pressed
with the weight of a foreign body on
your guts, clammy webbed feet scrabbling to get
a purchase; two or three rough jerks; a jet
of alien slime.   Don't get raped by a swan.

That's my advice. They said he was divine,
when they found me retching myself inside
out, afterwards, throwing up as if I'd
never stop. They said, treat it as a sign
of enviable favour. You're a myth,
now, they said; try to behave like one. Though
what I always wished, if you want to know,
was that I'd had something to hurt him with.

Jezebel to the Eunuchs

No priests. No tiring-women. If you please,
no pity, though I don't object to fear.
Furthermore, absolutely no
prophets, croaking 'I told you so.'
Lock up this turret room; give me the keys.
Vengeance can bloody come and get me here.
No prayers, reproaches, tears or homilies.
You three are privileged, you realise?
Marred men, whom nobody can mend,
you'll see how greatness makes its end –
even take part. You place your sympathies
where you want to; your Queen accepts she dies
in any case. You see that cloud of dust?
That's Jehu, driving like a lunatic.
Poor, god-pecked Jehu, comes to close
my wicked mouth for good. Ah, those
Jews, majestic tools of Yahweh! It must –
I can't believe it doesn't ever stick
in their throats, to grovel for such a god.
Pathetically obsessed with cleanliness,
their god. Well, just in case I meet
him: perfumed oil, to make me sweet
(no time for a bath now). You think this odd?
You'd dress for dinner, but you wouldn't dress
for death? I'll be prepared. Rouge, now, and kohl.
That smaller brush. Death: the greatest and last
of any woman's appointments –
surely the usual ointments
are not out of place – she should stay in rôle,
for fear of seeming to regret her past.
All past, the 'whoredoms, witchcrafts', sins and snares,
abominable to God. Or so they tell
me. Is he here yet? At the gate?
Oh, Jehu, Jehu – just too late.
Vengeance, that thinks to take me unawares
finds me ready, and looking...rather well.

Jael Discourses on Manners to the Corpse of Sisera

Long weariness of the same offence
could do it to anyone.
You find the limits of impotence
when all its patience is gone.
Then arrogance may plead ignorance –
plead mercy, there will be none.

Bad luck, I suppose you'd call it, when
you tread on a trodden thing;
it looks as though it were dead, but then
you suddenly feel the sting,
and point and poison and barb sink in…
A crawler can kill a king.

Bad luck, I suppose, Lord Sisera,
who commanded all your life,
that you fled from the field without a scar,
from internecine strife,
from your slaughtered hosts and your iron car,
to the tent of Heber's wife.

And *rotten* luck, that in all those years
when you ordered at your ease,
you never learned the smile that endears,
nor the Kenite word for 'Please' –
nor that hunted men, with foes and fears,
ask favours upon their knees.

With a tent-spike hammered through your head,
you're unlikely to understand
what it was you did, or seemed, or said,
to turn this generous hand
to murder. But listen, now you're dead:
I was not yours to command.

Did you take that tone with all you met?
I hadn't a lot to give;
I'm an unimportant woman. Yet
I would have let you live.
You have stained my carpet, red and wet,
with your careless imperative.

Calypso

I will have no more gifts from the gods, thank
you, after this one is taken from me.
Mine, but not mine. Then, only briefly mine;
poisoned and poisonous, like every gift
from the gods. Look, Calypso: here is love!

Nothing, I think, amuses them so much
as watching you seize your ruin, wide-eyed
with wondering gratitude – o, great gods!
Eternal life! (*But not eternal youth.*)
Invulnerability! (*Not quite entire.*)
Inhuman strength! (*Human stupidity.*)
A perfect love! (*Love, without permanence...*)

Only the gods can make their print that small.

So, after this – when he is gone from me,
back to the wife he never should have had –
no more surprises, thank you. Just the sea,
black rocks, red sunsets, gull-cries; everything
as it was before he came. Poisoned love.
One drop in the water of my solitude,
just one, to cloud its clarity forever,
leaving it tasting dull, like loneliness.

I will go to him now, and let him choose
for himself. I will make him say the words
that end it. 'Do you love her more than me?'
He will stare at the sand. He will mutter.
Something like, she is, after all, his wife.
I will be proud and beautiful, and say,
go to her – if you love her more than me.

I will be weak and cowardly. I'll come
laughing to bind his wrists up with my hair,
feed him with berries from my lips, and say,
'Love me for now. For one more human year.
For one more of your weeks. One little day.'

The sea looks limitless from here, unless,
like me, you know what eternity means.

No more gifts from the gods. Only, the right
to a fair hearing in your history.
Someone to say I never asked to be
the tawdry patron saint of Other Women
burning
in my temporary heaven.

Penelope

I know you've been with other women, though.
You never did that thing with my hair before.
Woman or witch, goddess or nymph – do you
really think it makes a difference to me?
Who had to wait for you through all these years
of undiluted chastity, or risk
earning the names of faithless wife and whore,
a blot on the bright scroll of your renown?
And I was courted, Odysseus, you know
I was. Not all of them displeased my eyes
(eyes of a normal woman, after all),
though some were rotten, and the rest were fools.
Not all were ugly, or unthinkable...
and I was courted. But that's over now.
As over as your great adventures are;
except that they will sing of you, and not
of me, unless to say I watched and wept
a loyal twenty years of life away.
The hell I did.
I did exactly what I wanted.
I disappeared inside myself, thinking
to the rhythm of my own thoughts,
weaving daydreams of wild doings
into a shroud
and then undoing it back to nothing...
so that it would be utterly,
gloriously pointless.
As futile as what you did.
As worthless as restore a worthless wife
back to the soured bed
of a husband who can hardly bear
to look at her lovely face any more.
As meaningless as every life ill lost
in doing so. And so many lives lost!
Entirely, splendidly pointless.

My darling. Good to have you back,
after so long;
the house rid of all those men who wanted me,
and life back to normal – my silent self,
my braggart husband and my pompous son.
No more of those long, lonely nights,
barely disturbed by the flutterings
of my nimble, weaving hands.
No more need for that.
I'm glad I kept our marriage-bed unspoilt;
you must be glad to lie in it again,
with your quiet pearl of a faithful wife.
I know you've been with other women.
That thing you did with my hair...

What Song the Syrens Sang

I genuinely wanted them to come.
It's most important that you understand
there was no malice in it. Only loss,
each time, and every time the loss was mine.
How could it have succeeded, otherwise?
Who embraces death on the strength of some
lukewarm invitation? No bald command,
no whore's cold patter gets a man to toss
his life away. Accident, not design,
flooded and burst their lungs; I sang no lies.

I never lied. I told them what I'd done,
each time. But who was listening to me?
I pointed out my island's grisly necklace
of wave-washed bones; sometimes I even cried,
sincerely, urgently, please, do not come!
On the knife horizon, the evening sun
slit his own throat and bled into the sea,
while they, the foolish, fascinated reckless,
jumped in to drown. I watched them as they died,
praying to all the gods to strike me dumb.

You understand, I had a job to do.
I did it very well – which doesn't mean
that I was ever satisfied. It was
no joy to me to see what I desired
struggle, fail, die, drift too late to my shore.
Why should I bother saying this to you?
Because in all my life I've never been
heard, when I warned 'I'm trouble.' Or because
I want you not to come to me. I'm tired.
I do not want to do this any more.